A PLACE AT THE TABLE

ALSO BY STEVE FOLEY

With the Hollow of Your Hand (poems)

A PLACE AT THE TABLE

Poems by

Steve Foley

Antrim House

Simsbury, Connecticut

Produced by Sheridan Books, Inc.

First Edition

2007

ISBN-13: 978-0-9770633-7-6

ISBN-10: 0-9770633-7-2

Library of Congress Control Number: 2006937597

Cover Painting by Milton Avery (1885-1965)

Child's Supper, 1945 (oil on canvas, 36 x 48 inches)

New Britain Museum of American Art

Gift of Roy R. Neuberger, 1954.32

Photo of the author by Diane Foley

Book & Cover Design by Rennie McQuilkin

Antrim House

www.antrimhousebooks.com

860.217.0023

ACKNOWLEDGEMENTS

Poems need guidance to discover what they are meant to be. My poems are the lucky godchildren of several truly wise counselors: Emily Holcombe, Rennie McQuilkin, Pam Nomura, Pit Pinegar, and above all, my teacher, Hugh Ogden, who opened the door and lit up the room.

Thanks to Candace Hall for permission to include poems published in *With the Hollow of Your Hand* (Andrew Mountain Press), and to the editors of *Friends' Journal*, *Northeast Magazine*, and *The Portland Review*, where some of the poems in this collection originally appeared. Thanks also to the New Britain Museum of American Art for permitting reproduction of Milton Avery's oil painting "Child's Supper."

To Diane, Lindsay and Justin:

you, who make poetry possible and life a blessing

A PLACE AT THE TABLE

I FIRST LOOK

II FINDING GRACE

A PLACE AT THE TABLE

III TRAVELERS

IV AS IF CALLED

A PLACE AT THE TABLE

V THE DRUMMER AND THE BUTTERFLY

VI AFTERWORD

VII ABOUT THE POET

Poets spend a lifetime hunting for the magic that will make the moment stay. — Stanley Kunitz

A PLACE AT THE TABLE

I

FIRST LOOK

When love comes to me and says
What do you know, I say This girl, this boy.

— Sharon Olds, "Looking at Them Asleep"

TO COLERIDGE

"And once, when he awoke in most distressful mood
I hurried with him to our orchard-plot,
And he beheld the moon and, hushed at once,
Suspended his sobs, and laughed most silently,
While his fair eyes, that swam with undropped tears,
Did glitter in the yellow moonbeam."

   —from "The Nightingale" by Samuel Taylor Coleridge

I have not yet held my son
up to the moon
to calm his nightmare cries
the way you offered up your Hartley.
Justin's fourth-month nights are all peace,
all blanketed sleep
in a dark broken only
by the sometime crack of hall light
as his mother or I
make certain of his beauty.

But when that night comes
and he scares me awake into his nightmare,
I will fumble through the dark,
take hold of him clutching me,
and introduce him to the moon,
to the silent voice of its light,

to the noiseless echo
of your son's tears
in the eyes of mine.

FIRST LOOK

Your brother and I sit playing on the rug,
pretending that sunlight forms a road for his car.
He stops,
looks up,
extends his open hand
to grab the dust that dances in the light,
then draws his fist,
smiling,
within inches of his eyes,
peeks in,
scowls,

bounds up,
thrusts both thirsting hands
into the light,
into the dust.

The door opens.
Your mother's home from Mount Sinai
where a sound wave machine has taken pictures of you.
She removes the single souvenir snapshot
from her pocketbook;
you've been outlined in white.

I see your full left profile,
gentle slope of your shoulders,
your arms, both legs.
I think I see one of your eyes.

When I hand you to your brother

he introduces you to sunlight.
You make our walls,
our ceiling,
shine.

THE ONE WHO NAMES

Wordless,
he tugs for me to follow; it's dark
and he wants to count the stars.
It's a game that pleases:
his rhythmic poking at the window,
my one two three four five.

But all this day
deserts of snow have blown past this window,
dissolving into outline most of what we know,
and tonight
there is only one star.

When he points I say
one.
After straining for the others,
he looks briefly to me,
then back to the sky.
He pokes the black pane where a second should shine,
then another,
another.
I am mum
and soon the one star is gone.

On tiptoe,
palms flat against glass,
he fixes on the spot where the light had shone
and calls to it,
calls again,
offering up its name.

THE SOURCE

For what seems like hours
my fingertips hover like divining rods
above these arid keys,
waiting for signs of a buried poem.
Still
no hint of a strike.

From her room
the gurgling of my baby daughter.

I lift her from her crib,
lay her on the rug and lie beside her.
While she reports her day's news
I reach to wipe water from her chin.

With her whole right hand
she clutches my ring finger,
with her left my pinky,
for a moment suspends them just above her eyes,
then yanks them to her lips
to suck.

She sucks to learn what my fingers can tell her,
what it is they seek,
what it is they know,
sucking hard, determined,
until she is certain that all they hold is hers,

then she releases them,
closes both eyes,
and replaces my fingers with her own.

THE ROAD

Absorbed in the perils of *Starsky and Hutch*,
I ignore his Camaro
until it's idling at the crest of my knee.

Like a Sunday driver
he pokes along the boulevard
posing as my thigh,
bears left at my belt loop,
hard right at the buckle,
then puts the pedal down due north.
At the right shoulder off-ramp
he decelerates,
yielding,
awaiting his opportunity to nose into the flow.
Once he's meandered to the edge of my shirt cuff
he executes a U-turn
in a no U-turn zone,
so I snatch his hand,
Chevy and all,
and hold on.

He tugs.
I maintain.
He contorts.
I insist.
He sinks,
he rises,
wriggles,
pirouettes;
he hops,

he shimmies,
to no avail.

Seconds pass without movement.
When our eyes meet
we smile,
each certain the other
will let go.

HER FAVORITE GAME

is Slip Away.
She's been playing it now
for quite some time
in one form or another.

This round starts with me in the recliner,
focused on the latest from CBS News,
until she sneaks into my lap,
wraps her arms around my neck
and digs her flushed cheek into my chest.

Eyes shut tight, brow shining,
lips a bit apart,
she lies still as sleep,
like one floating at dawn
on a pristine lake,
each breath a gentle swell.
I smooth her hot hair
with the flat of my hand,

but just when my arms
wrap securely around her
they are empty
and she's racing,
squealing out the door.

WHAT HE KNOWS

Even the sun is falling.

This day we have been children together.
Coats empty on porch steps,
we've lost each other in heaps of spent leaves,
shaken dead stems from the tangles in our hair,
shouted joy across the yards of fenced neighbors;
this is that day in all Octobers
when the summer reminds us
of its leaving.

Now, we lie still.
Shadows cold across our bodies,
leaves mute beneath our backs,
I watch November push the light into houses
and devise an oral quiz for him
to find out what he knows.

"Why, do you suppose, all the leaves have fallen?"

"I think there are a few more left."

HIS CAT LIFE

His name, he claims,
is Huckle.
Huckle Cat.
He's a cat for breakfast,
a cat for snack,
a cat for Halloween.

He stands rapt in the supermarket
before a box of tabby treats,
curls up on a cushion,
licks dirt from both front paws.

Instead of crying when he falls
he meows.

Then one gray day he watches Annabel
from next door
steal across our back yard,
leaping patches of spring snow,
a blue jay flopping from her jaws.

His name, he claims,
is Huckle.
Huckle Bear.

THIRTIETH BIRTHDAY

He sits strapped behind me
as I churn against the constant wind
of a dying afternoon.
No downslopes left,
no stretches of rest,
only the steady rise toward home.

The breeze burns water into each eye
and the sun reddens my abandoned scalp.
Air in the lungs proves hard to come by,
harder to hold once it's there.

In short bursts
comes his voice,
only when I exhale.

"Someday

bike I want

four seats

red wheels

four sets

bars

buy bike

race it

front seat

mine."

ICARUS

Kneeling,
he drags his cupped hand smoothly
through the playground sand.
"A road, Daddy!"
I smile,
check my watch that isn't there,
settle for a guess from the position of the sun.

Above the western tree line,
a hang glider,
now a second,
smaller,
just behind.
They drift apart,
both rising with a gentle roundness
like the outermost limbs of a seasoned oak,

then rush headlong at one another,
converging on the sun,
only to climb by intersecting circles,
one ring above the other,
taut, like braided hair.

I look down at him.
He's stopped his digging to watch.
"Someday I'll grow big,
even bigger than you,
and bang my head against the sky."

SOCCER SATURDAY

On the ride to the playing field
he vows to kill Green.
"If Green gets even any goals
Orange will get mad,
and when Orange gets mad,
Orange kills."
In her seat beside him
she reads to her bear.

For nearly an hour Orange kicks,
Green kicks,
no one scores.
Under a maple
she colors,
keeping neatly in the lines,

and after Orange has announced
that it appreciates Green,
she runs hard to me,
calling out across the empty field.

With unbroken stride she leaps into the air,
certain I will catch her.
"Higher!" she commands me,
so I toss her above me,
time after time,
catch her at her sides
until she arches so far,
knees dug into my shoulders,
her back a quarter moon,

that I can barely hang on,

then she's down again,
off again,
turning cartwheel after cartwheel,
enough to fill the sky.

UP TO YOU

It's up to you,
now that you walk straight
to first grade every nine a.m.,
line up in the playground,
file in,
sit down to learn the sounds of vowels,
to understand that things add up,
that things can be taken away,

emerge later on
to face hallway bullies,
rules of the library,
hot lunch,

only to strap on your backpack at three,
tuck your chin to spite the headwind
and beat the bus home;

yes it's up to you,
now that a gale-blown starling
lies dazed in our window box,
not remembering her course for the leafless maple,
not remembering her perch on the wire,

to disinter your sewn cardinal
buried in your closet,
seam unraveling at one wing,
to show it full on your side of the window,
thrust it high to make it soar,
make it dip

and glide,

because it's you
who must remind the starling
how to fly.

TRYING TO SLEEP IN MY SON'S BED

Too short, too narrow,
too much give at the spine.
At my feet a stuffed panther,
cartoon pillowcase under my head.
Where I should, he sleeps,
stretched out beside his mother.
I listen to his measured breathing,
double up the pillow at the base of my neck.
Above me a plaster crack,
jagged, diagonal.
Is it ever lightning to him
here in the half-light,
seconds ticking down the hall?
Is that coat rack ever the Wicked Witch of Oz?

No answers this night.
No comfort,
until, in the hallway,
my daughter, trembling,
her nightmare refusing to let go.
"Lindsay, honey, I'm here.
Here."

She runs to me.
Only my arms will do,
only my lips on her long sweet hair,
its color unmatched
but for that instant in the sky
when the earth
with what love
accepts the sun.

GEOGRAPHY

for Diane

At the head of our driveway
stands Canada in chalk,
at the center the USA.
Just south of Jersey sits France.
Everywhere in white
loom road signs, highways, ramp garages, lots.
A car conquers continents in seconds,
its driver alive
in the voice of a child.

Our car waits in the street.

After dinner our living room
becomes New New York,
capital of Lego Land,
a snap-together town house at one end of Main Street,
stretching to the fix-it shop just shy of the recliner
and two feet from a farm.

All evening long we have straddled this metropolis,
tiptoed quietly along the outskirts of town,

but night falls,

and while our children dream
what they still have left to dream of,
we clear ourselves space
and make love on our living room floor.

II

FINDING GRACE

*If the present is all we have, then the present
lasts forever.* — Anne Lamott, *Plan B*

THE TWILIGHT LEAGUE

to my father

Sonny Thomas lashes a rope to left-center,
looks up rounding second,
coasts into third. He could run forever
if he only had the room.
The spitfire Proctor twins,
one at short, one at second,
turn a sure one-out single
into a slam-bang double play.
It's Valco versus Hamilton Standard,
the summer of '60 in dusty Colt Park,
a battle for first in the Twilight League.

At the end of seven
it's too late to play the nine,
so we climb into the Biscayne,
head home to have a catch out back.

I take my spot, worn through to bare earth,
rub spit into the pocket of my Johnny Logan glove,
tug twice on the bill of my Cleveland cap.
You start me with a grounder.
I stab, whirl, fire,
watch as you retrieve it from under the porch.
You decide to try me on high flies.

Already you are fifty,
short of breath, trifocaled,
so stiff with bursitis you can barely lift your arm.

Already you sleep in a twin bed.
Still, as the falling night erases everything around us,
you hurl that ball just as high as you can
so that I can take advantage of last light.

MATINEE AT THE WEBSTER

for Weasel

The second feature over,
we skirt the lobby with the parent come to fetch us
and slip out the back way.
November dusk in the city;
the cool will see us home.

Once we've rounded the corner
we stop running,
look back;
no sign.
Unzipped jackets flapping loose at our hips,
stocking caps jammed in the bottoms of pockets,
we grin at our being
anonymous on Julius Street.

We leap low hedges
separating properties,
tightrope iron railings,
hunch beside cars,

crash phone booths
scale chain links
punch doorbells
light Luckies
chuck rocks
chalk sidewalks
dodge buses
swear clouds.

This is the air that is meant to be breathed.

But soon, there it is:
the neon Flying A lighting up our corner.
Nothing left to do
but zip up,
pull our caps on,
settle on a story
and straight-arrow home.

PAYING THE RENT

Old Lady Wilman's lips part slightly,
come together again.
No color in them,
no more than in her cheeks
or in her hair against the pillow.
Little air in her bedroom,
little light, even though the sun is fierce
on this last day of July.

Behind me stands my father,
hands on my shoulders.
He's always come here on his own before,
but this month he's been told
to bring his youngest son.

His thumbs inch me forward.
"Lean in a bit, Stephen," he murmurs.
"Mrs. Wilman has something important to say."

Her eyelids flutter,
lips break apart.
I hear her breathing,
each exhale like an underwater bubble
rising to free the sound trapped inside.
Angled forward,
arms at my sides,
I hover there forever,
until she raises one hand inches off the bed,
and suddenly, it's time for us to go.

Walking to our car,
my father rubs one hand
on the top of my head
and with the other slips a dollar
in my shirt-front pocket,
money I can spend
however I please.

EMMETT, TINY TRAVELER, ON HIS BACK IN THE LIVING ROOM

As if the air were his only itinerary
he pedals, arms cycling independently
of legs, no obstacles in his way
on this, his seventh Wednesday.
While he rides he gurgles,
bubbles and babbles,
maybe telling his life story,
or the impressions he can summon
of the day he was born:

wet warmth of the birthing tub

first whoosh, then roar

muted light

snap of separation

air, no air

air, no air.

Then he stops mid-syllable,
arms up,
legs down,
like he's risen to the crest of a hill he's been climbing
and decided to coast in silence for a while.

THIRD BIRTHDAY

for Jason

Chocolate
calls the candy dish
from way across the living room.
The rest of us can only hear
January wind rattling the windows,
but his only sound is
Chocolate,

so he scrambles to his father's side
to whisper in his ear.
"You've had enough,"
is what he's told.
"You'll spoil your dinner."

But no other words are as loud as
Chocolate,

so he waits for what he knows must be longer than a lifetime,
then shuts his eyes
to become invisible
and makes his way smiling,
answering the call.

AT THE RED LIGHT

For everyone else
it's an order to stop,
for us
permission.
Through two car windows
we say hello.
His eyes remind me of an old picture of my brother.

His mother inches forward,
anxious for the green,
but I move up to stay close.
He raises an oversized hockey helmet,
new, protective,
and presses it against the glass.
I mug astonishment,
deepest admiration,
and stretch to get a look at what else
he can produce.

First comes a ski hat.
Then a snow brush
and rusty de-icer can.
Two blue mittens.
A boot.

The light changes.

Gradually, the distance
between us grows.
I spot his head bobbing, searching

for one more,
one last to get hold of,

then he turns onto a side street
and fades
like the photo from Christmas morning,
my brother smiling in his Davy Crockett cap,
tree lights echoing in his eyes.

A QUAKER WEDDING, JULY

Silence is the enemy of children,
the warning shot of sleep
and missing out,
so when Reverend Holcombe sends us
into quiet contemplation
and all is hushed,
one tiny, plaintive whisper drifts over us,
like the breeze above the ancient elms
shading this sweltering Meeting House.

On a bench beside his father, a child of five
corkscrews to the floor, then rises
to emphasize the seriousness of his thirst.
Top button buttoned, the knot of his tie
seems half the size of his face,
scarlet from the heat and the strain
of being good.
He lurches,
gets reeled in,
the rub of "I love you" at the small of his back,
the tug of "Behave" at his wrist.

The bride and groom now rise
to stand before us,
holding hands.
They promise to cherish
each moment of solitude,
every second spent in company,
to love with equal measure
both silence and sound.

The boy shuts his eyes,
slumps shapeless across his father's leg,
lips moving to an improvised,
inaudible song.

THE BOY FROM THE OPPORTUNITY
ROOM, 1962

Oh, how we envy him his shadow,
ample in comparison to the flagpole's sliver
knifing across the narrow clump of green
that rings this school.
It's 2:53. Eternity extends
between the rest of us
and dismissal,
yet there he is, outside already,
face lifted to the sun,
arms raised at sharp angles,
hands grasping the once white rope,
poised to bring to earth again
the American flag.

None of us in this sixth-grade class know his name,
where he lives,
or what he does up there all day,
he and those others tucked away
in that third floor corner room,
past art,
past music,
past the closet marked "Storage,"
up there behind that heavy, windowless door
that nobody's seen open,
that nobody's ever been sent to with a message.

All we know is that he and the others
are gathered daily in a school bus,
dropped off once we're all inside,

sit together in the lunchroom,
play together in the yard,
and trail out toward the waiting bus
before the ending bell,

that one of them can barely see,
another wears the same dress every day,
another is an albino,
another has a hand that faces backward,
and that every rainless day,
while we copy the names of Supreme Court Judges,
or recite the chief exports of Chile and Peru,
this same tall boy
and his long, attendant shadow
grab hold of our flag,
snap it hard to get the snags out,
and bring together those corners
that are farthest apart.

PICTURE FOR SALE IN
THE MYSTIC GIFT SHOP

Lucky Billy,
blue eyes brimming,
clean cloth cap just as blue,
hands cocked with confidence
above his right ear,
fine bat of ash at the ready,
his smile every bit as white

as Our Savior's,
right behind Billy,
His face a head taller,
capless, hair flowing,
flowing robe, sleeves slack below the wrists
as He bolsters Billy's grip,
the pitch on its way,
no sign of doubt in either set of eyes.

Let us pity, then, the non-believers,
alone in the batter's box,
doomed to swing and miss,
not once but three times over,
while Billy sends one
up above the clouds,
then flies around the bases,
barely seeming
to be in contact
with the ground.

SKATING IN THE CEMETERY

to Jessica at 9

I sit beside you on the bench
just left of the Colson plot
as you lace up quick
and sure.
The wheels these days are slick polyvinyl
instead of nicked metal,
and the shoes lace high,
tight and trim.
These skates are built for style,
built for speed.

You stand, push off,
circumscribe the tarred figure-eight
that snakes among the headstones,
keeping low in the turns,
within yourself,
conservative,
but flat-out on the straight-aways,
jacket like a sail,

too fast
to read inscriptions,
to subtract date of birth
from date of death,
to wonder what happened to Emily Haworth,
1823 to 32,

too fast to return the wave I offer
as you race against no one
on this, the anniversary
of the day you were born.

DOUBLE DUTCHER

The ropes snap whipcracks
as she waits outside their arc
rocking on the playground tar.
She leans in
away
in
away
in,
until the ends
seem to be turning
her.
In
away
in
away.

In.

The sun, too, beats the blacktop
and her feet reject the tar as if it were the sun itself.
Nothing else moves,
just wrists
ropes
her feet.

The ends chant a tale
about the names of states
about the names of stars
about the names of boys
who will love her.
The rope that trips her

is the boy she will marry.
The ropes have always tripped her at
Robert or William,
have always put an end to the rhythm
with a name,

but today she times the turns
just right
just right

and strides away smiling
with the ropes still whirling.

ANGEL

sings in my classroom
until I tell her no —
Christmas carols,
TV jingles,
the latest from Madonna,
each note light like a piccolo played cleanly
on a hill above a stream,

and when I pass out books to read Shakespeare aloud
she commandeers the star part
and makes Juliet sing
a Capulet cantata of whole note *prithees*,
quarter note *wherefores*,
banishèds in scat,

and with the signal of the bell
Angel whistles out the doorway,
hums her locker combination,
gives voice to the hallway on her path to the bus
that will haul her out of town,
past stockaded yards full of in-ground pools,
tiled patios, flowers,

haul her on the highway
headed to the city,
as far as her block,
where some buildings have windows,
some windows have glass,
where some stairwells have no one
fast asleep on them,

where some apartment doors
aren't identified in chalk,
where some living rooms have heat,
where some fathers live at home,

where Angel, undoubtedly,
sings well into the night.

IN AMSTERDAM AT SEVENTEEN

All I know of this girl, Anne Frank,
comes from twenty minutes of her movie
while the Mets game I'd tuned in to watch
was delayed by rain.
Mostly I remember Shelley Winters whining.

There isn't much to look at on the main floor,
so I climb the narrow stairs
once hidden by a bookcase
to the attic on display.
I'm relieved not to find the squeaky clean guide
I've come to expect as standard equipment,
just a few fellow tourists
going through the motions.
The place looked bigger on TV.

As I back up to avoid a herd of browsing Texans,
the corner of something wedges between my shoulder blades.
I turn

to Ginger Rogers,
Ray Milland,
preserved behind glass,
their clipped edges almost touching each other,
and suddenly I'm standing where Anne stood
as she oh so carefully so they would not tear
smoothed the paper faces of these people of her dreams,
leaned back to gaze at them,
speak for them,
sing to them,

marry them
before she was taken,

standing where there are no salesmen,
no experts on the subject,
only my eyes where hers had been,
smiling at the stars.

DIRTY MICHAEL

I let the water run
hot only
enough to steam the mirror
lather hard
between the fingers
under nails
down in creases where it hides
three times every time
has to be three
work that bar
like a blade
'til they're raw
'til they sting from any contact
even from the air

three times three
three times every day
three weeks running
three times three times three

still
everyone sees it
as soon as they look at me
they have to
they pretend
but they can't miss it
I can tell by their eyes

so I run the hot only
make the glass steam good

work that Ivory as deep as I can
three times three

so deep that when I go outside any time it's raining
they lather up
on their own

EVACUATION

The blare of his horn
cuts through the alarm,
grows nearer as I wait at our prearranged spot
beside the far bank of lockers
on the school's second floor.
No drill this time.
The real thing,
smoke billowing from the boys' bathroom door.

I see him now,
his eyes on mine,
finger on the forward switch of his chair.
I kneel to unstrap him,
cinched like a sack on a grocery push cart,
my free palm at his sternum
to keep him from toppling.
I place his hands in his lap,
reach under his thighs,
around his back
and lift.
"Jesus," I think, "there's nothing left to him."
I shoulder through the fire doors,
make sure of my grip,
and start down,
shifting him at the landing
to keep him from slipping away.
He can't help,
can't put his arms around my neck
to hang on.

Once outside
we struggle to the site
set aside for his evac chair.
No one's brought it.
My palms sweat.
I swing around and around,
like a soldier,
wounded buddy in his arms,
desperate for a medic
or the sound of chopper blades on high.

I say, "Hang on, Matt.
Everything's okay.
The chair's coming.
I'll hold you 'til it does."

But my body can't lie.
It tells him, "Soon you'll be too much for me.
I can't keep you from the ground for very long."

I raise a knee to the small of his back,
lean our weight against the outer gym wall.
He angles his head to see my face.
"We'll be fine," he tells me.
"We've gone far enough.
There's nothing more that you can do."

HER PAPERBACK GATSBY

for Emily, paralyzed by a drunk driver on her graduation night

The phrases underlined in fine point blue
refuse to grant me the irony I seek.
How many years now, eight,
ten since she dog-eared the corner of 135?
Since she snapped back the binding
so the pages would lie flat while she read,
legs slowly scissor-kicking air?
Was it the last book she studied
before her commencement,
before she ran to her car,
done up in streamers,
some maroon,
some gold,
heading for the party to dance the night away?

Now, all these years later
I find, by chance, her copy in the book room,
her small, neat name printed just inside its cover,
and repair to my desk
in search of hard solace.
Somehow it will help if she's highlighted,
"They were careless people, Tom and Daisy —
they smashed up things and creatures
and then retreated…"
or "Tomorrow we will run faster,
stretch our arms farther."

But she hasn't,

and I can't even say for sure
that she loved this book,
that its poetry thrilled her,

or that when she arrived at the very last line
she understood what it means to be adrift
in this current, ceaselessly bearing us back
into the past.

THE END OF OCTOBER

A ghost comes to my door tonight, Jessie.
"Trick or treat!" she shouts,
and as I plop a wrapped candy into her bag
I try to picture you at six or seven,
as a clown maybe, yarn for hair
and a squirting flower,
or as a pirate with an eye patch,
one blackened tooth and a hook for a hand.

Back inside, I sit at the table
where we gathered last Christmas,
the rest of us savoring our turkey, sweet potatoes,
our cookies and our pie,
while the flame of one thin candle
shadowed the empty plate set down before you,
flickered its reflection
off your half-filled Diet Coke glass,
unnecessary napkin still folded in your lap.

It's the first Halloween
since your heart gave out on you at twenty-two,
since your mother stood before us in the pulpit
and read the poem I wrote the day you turned nine,
the day you took me by the hand
through the lengthening shadows
up the cemetery path,
where I sat and watched you skate
at break-neck speed around the walkway,
your jeans rolled up almost to your knees,
shouting "Watch this!"

when you reached the long slope down.
And later when I asked you
how you thought of skating there,
you told me, "This is the place
where all us kids go."

Again the doorbell rings.
If you were here, Jessie,
in the light outside my doorway,
eyes smiling,
pigtails bobbing on either side,
I wouldn't care what you were wearing.
I wouldn't ask what way you came.
I'd just offer you the candy bowl,
let you rake in all the best ones,
all the sweetest you could find.

FINDING GRACE

I search my neighbor's weed patch,
thigh high on me, but over her head
if Grace were in it.
No sign,
no glint of late September sun
glancing off blonde hair,

and I'm rushed back twenty years ago,
wading through a field this wild,
shouting my niece's name.
Jessie!
Jessica! We found her that day
but lost her two years ago.

I try behind a maple
then a tangle of bushes,
an unlocked shed.
Grace echoes through the neighborhood,

when all at once there's laughter,
cries of joy,
applause,
so I run toward her white Cape four houses down
and see her sitting on her front steps,
people hugging all around her,
red juice from a Popsicle streaming down her chin.
"She was safe the whole time," someone announces,
curled up in her closet,
oblivious to us all.

I take a seat beside her,
tousle her hair.
She reaches for my nose,
presses it.
"Beep," I say, so she does it again.
I beep even louder,
finding refuge in her smile.

III

TRAVELERS

*If it's darkness
we're having, let it be extravagant.*

— Jane Kenyon, "Taking Down the Tree"

THE DENTIST'S WAITING ROOM

At first there is only a fedora beside me,
an island of cream on a brown vinyl chair,
but soon its owner's back from x-ray
to lift it by the brim,
place it gingerly on the carpet,
sit down to read *Time*.

His shoes, too, are cream,
and his thin nylon hose,
summer weight slacks.
All cream.
But his shirt,

his shirt's an explosion,
a festooning of flowers,
marigold, peony,
geranium, rose,
and tulip upon tulip,
tumultuous like fireworks against a starless sky,
his face pure serenity above the silent uproar,
lips barely moving as he reads.

When the hygienist comes to claim him
he plucks the fedora,
returns it to the chair,
then winks at me solemnly,
hand on my shoulder,
lips to my ear.
"My teeth are my own," he says,
"every last one."

FEBRUARY SUNSET, MYRTLE BEACH

The way Spanish moss drapes from cypress branches
her sleeves hang below her outstretched arms,
palms up,
fingers divining the horizon.
Trade winds flap her long, white hair,
balloon her shapeless shift,
the color of the sea oats swirling behind her,
while waves threaten her toe-hold in the sand.
Two paces to her left
her walker awaits,
front wheels twisted to keep it
from blowing away.

She drops one arm,
then the other,
gently to her thighs,
then raises both at once to either side,
like a mast,
like the gull that glides above the whitecaps,
barely visible in the fading light.

She shuts her eyes
and inhales deeply,
deeply,
securing every scrap
of available air,
then exhales like a bellows
enlivening a tired fire.

Again and again,

the drawing in,
the easing out,
as if her clouds of breath are gifts she's sending to a loved one
whose ship sails on that ocean,
on its way toward rest
in some half-remembered port
on the far side of the world.

PRESENT PERFECT

for Helen

She can easily locate
the one that shows her in her uniform,
smiling,
though she swears she only played
when her team was way ahead
or way behind.

And the day her second girl was born?
No problem —
a cloudless third of May,
cooler than normal,
storms the night before
clearing humid air away.

Those pop up plain as day,
without effort,
every etched detail exactly as she remembers it,
exactly as she narrates it
every time,

but she cannot
for the life of her
find the one that confirms
this morning's cup of coffee,

the one that will show her nagging daughters
that yes she did

take her Thursday pill on Thursday
and not Wednesday afternoon.

And where is her car key?
How can she play her numbers
without her car?
The car she used just yesterday,
she's practically sure of it,

though she can't quite see it,
not the way she sees her young smile,
second from the left,
second row standing,
number twenty-four.

HIS FALL

He missteps at the threshold
between living and dining room,
cane catching at the ridge of blue carpet,
free hand clutching at the air.
She lunges,
grabs one sleeve below the elbow,
a handful of belt,
but his fall is already too far underway.

For a moment they lie tangled,
her foot caught up under him,
before she frees herself, jimmies him
until his back's against a wall
so she can kiss his cheek,
wipe both eyes,
tease him about frightening the neighbors down below.

Only when she's fed him lunch
and eased him into his afternoon nap
does she open the freezer,
wrap ice in a face cloth,
apply it to her ankle
gone purple and black.

A BODY IN MOTION

for David

tends to stay in motion,
a body at rest,
at rest,
Newton's second law.
A given,

like the odds of every coin flip
remaining fifty-fifty,
no matter how many times
it comes up heads.
A constant,

like heat always rising,
positive forces always repelling,
every pushed object always pushing back
in return.
All these you believe.
All these you teach.

So when the good heart of your strong friend fails
to stay in motion,
what is there to do

but sit before your desk
in the science teachers' workroom
and stare into the quarter-eaten muffin,
picked clean of berries,

squeezing the remains
of your crumpled paper napkin,
refusing to let go.

AT JEFFERSON CONVALESCENT

for Dick Buckley

His tide's almost out.
I wait bedside for his next shallow breath,
his eyelids sagging.
At last it arrives,
but not the next word
of the sentence he's left hanging.
He only gets one now,
breath or memory.

I walk to the window.
The floodlit lot's nearly empty,
the hillside beyond it shadowed in twilight.
Above them, rain swollen clouds,

and I remember the gale thirty-five years ago,
waves of rain battering our walls,
flickering candle by my bed,
straining to hear Dick's voice,
my father's laughter,
the slap of plastic cards on the kitchen table.

Louder rain, fiercer wind,
the worst crack of thunder.
Then the scrape of his chair
as he pushed back from the table,
the screen door moaning,
holding still,
banging shut,
his wife's exasperated call:

"Come back in here, Richard,
you'll be struck by lightning!"
And in the tone he'd use
to shake me with laughter:
"You know, Gert dear, I do believe
we might be in for rain."

I turn from the window.
His heavy eyes have followed me.
Reflected in the painted flowers
hanging on the wall above him,
one more flash of the coming storm.

YOUR FATHER'S DEATH

for Tony

By the third ring
you are awake, by her fourth word
up, in your pajamas,
barefoot.

Driving, you list his previous attacks,
assign a date to each one.
From their driveway you see the kitchen curtain
drop, the back hall light
flick on.

She leads you to him,
nods at the space between bed and dresser.
He wears one sock,
striped boxers.
You slip your hands beneath him,
think better of it,
press two fingers to the base of his throat.

Arriving in silence,
the paramedics inspect him,
lift him to the gurney,
negotiate the turns
on the way to the front door.

You stay one step behind,
lend a hand at the landing,
stand empty-handed at the curb

then pace
back and forth
until you realize you're running,
running and yelling,
soon, only yelling.

The ambulance is gone.
You climb behind the wheel
and follow.

FOREIGN WAR

His name,
or all I can pronounce of it,
is Nha.
He's fifteen,
just arrived,
knows no English.
He is from the boats that fled Saigon
where his mother, two sisters,
remain. Today,
in a seat by a window
in the last row of my classroom,
he attends my explanation
of the participial phrase.
His eyes never move,

like your eyes, Dad,
in August of '70,
my brother in 'Nam,
you in St. Francis,
Room 417,
staring at the ceiling,
left hand tight around the bedrail.
I read aloud Mark's letter from Chu Lai.
Your eyes never move

as he cheerfully greets you,
assures you of his safety,
guarantees your swift recovery,
acknowledges,

in closing,
his desire to be home.

"This is not my home,"
the eyes say.
"These are not my clothes.
I understand
nothing."

A BREAK IN THE SILENCE, ROOM 440A

Ashamed of the stain on his fitted sheet,
of the odor his life makes, leaking away,
my dad can't face me.
I exhibit great interest in his row of Hallmark cards.
From behind the drawn curtain
bisecting the room
comes a single word,
"No!"

Then a pause,
then the word again,
sharper,
followed by another,
each disembodied negative
more plaintive than the last.
My father trembles,
planes the top of his head with the flat of one hand,
makes himself look at me, imploring with his eyes.

"Can I help?" I ask the curtain.
No end to the sound.
I step out into the hallway.
No sign of an attendant.
No aide.

When I go back inside
my dad has raised up on one elbow,
swiping at the curtain,
coming nowhere near,

until he slumps back with a thud,
eyes tied now to the ceiling,
pounds the iron bedrails,
shouts the single word
"Yes!"

MORTICIAN AT THE ADDING MACHINE

With lean, unerring fingers
he tabulates the costs.
Five death certificates – fifteen dollars.
Thirty for the forest green canopy by the grave.
Church money,
limo money,
coffin money,
vault,

and because the plot in question
has been paid for in advance,
there's a ten percent reduction
off the standard final sum.

The final sum
of a man who worked insurance forty-one years,
who drove second-hand Chevys,
never owned a home,

who would never raise his voice in anger,
who hummed before the shaving mirror,
whistled Mills Brothers' tunes as he dried the dinner dishes,

who the last few years grew resigned in the recliner,
who'd lift his shoe to my knee when his laces came undone,
who dreamed of once again
being able to sign his own name,

who watched me from his bed at Manchester Memorial
as I fished for my car keys,
telling him what time I would visit tomorrow,
then took hold of me with his hands and eyes
and said, "Stephen, don't tell your mother,
but I just don't think I'm going to last the night."

TRAVELERS

It's the one my mother,
now 80,
loves most, my father centered,
smiling in his office chair,
my brother and I like bookends on his desk,
she in the background with her solid dress.
Not yet four, my grin is unstudied,
seems to stretch to its echo on my father's face.
Mark and our mother share the same eyes.

She makes sure I see it every time I bring her groceries,
makes the very same comments,
week in, week out,
that the photo was taken on his silver anniversary,
that she'd clipped it from the pages of *The Travelers' Beacon*,
that I was always the one
who could make my dad laugh.

Next comes the one she keeps right beside it,
though it was taken before both Mark and I were born:
the two of them in a dim Manhattan bar,
he in uniform, she in gabardine,
neither capable of producing a smile.
"The next day he was shipped overseas," she says.
"Our first baby had died just a little before.
They never showed him to me in the hospital.
You can see we're not happy.
We don't know if we'll ever
see each other again."

A PLACE AT THE TABLE

to John, who died in infancy

Every Christmas for years
I've picked a spot beneath the tree
for the gift I would have given you,
another in the driveway for your car,
and at our table, a setting,
my son to your right, daughter to your left,
our mother directly across.
For years it's been my secret,
but someday, when I'm ready,
I'll stop and tell the children where I've placed you,
show Mother where you are

just as she revealed to me last Memorial Day,
standing beside me at Rose Hill,
Lot Number 8,
saying, "This is where the baby is,
our first one, John,"
pointing to her place for you that no one recognizes,
no dated stone,
no record of the breaths you took,
just a foot-square patch of well kept grass,
Grandpa Foley to the right of you,
Grandma to your left,
as if some terror in the night
had led you to seek comfort in their bed,

and Mother beside me,
brushing away a stray leaf with the rubber tip of her cane,
as though it were a crumb left on your cheek,
or a speck of dust
settled in your hair.

WEIGHING MY MOTHER

Because she's lost interest in the food of this world
two aides slip the canvas sling beneath her,
behind her shoulders first,
her spine,
until it reaches her tailbone,
the backs of her thighs.
Then one turns the crank just enough to raise her,
while the other jots the verdict on a chart.
For weeks they've tried to lure her with favorites:
lemon-lime sherbet,
tapioca pudding,
hot fudge.
At first she'd agree,
even lift the lid from the plastic container,
but lately she won't even part her lips to say no.

Now, limbs hanging low,
head lolling,
she's little more than freight
above a dockyard pier,

or maybe
another sort of new arrival
transported by air,
her pouch of white cloth cradled,
enormous white wings spread wide above her,
oh so close to being delivered.

IV

AS IF CALLED

Some part of art is the art
of waiting — the chord
behind the tight fence
of a musical staff.

—Ted Kooser, "Four Civil War
Paintings by Winslow Homer"

NOD ROAD, EARLY MAY

I want to be lean and hard for once,
so I up the gear to its highest resistance
and push along the blacktop toward Bel Campo.

The high school crew drives its shell alongside of me,
oars entering the Farmington together,
no splash.
Each stroke starts in the gut,
ends at the small of the back.
Good; the tops of my thighs
are beginning to tighten.

There's practice, too, at Metacon Gun,
shotgun shooters tracking clay
and squeezing,
shoulders kicking with each blow.
Pain now
behind my rib cage,
the right pain,
the one I'm after,
the kind I'm sure will serve me well.

Then, just around the curve,
a beat-up compact by the side of the road.
Mud brown body,
pea green door on the driver's side.
The man at the wheel
pours wine in plastic glasses.
A woman faces him,
her back to the vinyl dash.

I see them toast
then drain their glasses,
fill them again to toast a second time.

To shade perhaps.
To stillness.
To this very moment.
To things as they are.

RANGELEY LAKES POEMS

for Hugh Ogden

Fallen from the dock
the just-typed pages float face up,
until the clipboard that binds them bobs,
begins its plunge.
Flat on your chest you fish them out,
peel one from the other,
lay them on slats
in the June Maine sun.

You pace,
halt,
light a smoke,
kneel down,
check your watch against the contest deadline,
the hour they must be posted.
They dry far too slowly,
now that Rangeley has claimed them,
now that they are of
what they'd only been about —

of the still lake water
that mirrored the lone osprey
as it narrowed its slow circle
in search of its next meal,

that dripped from your oar blade,
poised above the surface,
as you skimmed in silence among channels in the reeds,

straining for the slightest trace of moose.

Yes they dry too slowly,
so you sweep them to you
and clamber for your car,
breathless for the nearest stretch of straight road.

Windows wide,
pedal flush with the floor,
you thrust each sheet into wind you manufacture,
each christened poem
unfurling as you fly.

AS IF CALLED

They've come down this morning from melt-swollen streams
to the edge of this thoroughfare,

to the grit left from snowfalls
now pushed into piles along both shoulders,

to dandelioned railroad beds
grown wild, to sprouts sprung up

through cracks in the macadam
at the abandoned drive-in movie lot.

They stand statue still,
no puff of breath above them,

no lifting of a foreleg
or flicking of an upright ear,

no sign of understanding in their eyes
as they watch this sunrise rush

toward insurance, toward accounting
for every dollar earned and spent

by everyone everywhere for everything,
imprinted on machines to which we've handed over memory.

Yes today
from greening hills

they have come down in wonder,
as if called.

BAT IN THE WOOD STOVE, JULY

It must have felt inviting,
that first cool line of brick
just beyond the reach
of three p.m. sun,

and even cooler at the smoke shelf,
swept clean of ashes,
or on the ridge of cast iron,
dormant since late March.

But the best must have come
once inside the firebox,
hanging from the damper rod,
kite-wings tucked,
oblivious to preparations
beyond the latched doors.

Later,
after the flame of bunched paper,
broken tree,
the ashes of bat are indiscernible
from the rest.

EYE IN THE SKY

We see them from the chopper—
flood victim waving from a shingled island,
suspect surrounded,
spread-eagled on the tar,

bridge jumper in the heartland,
freed hostages in flight.

That August day so many years ago,
as I cut across a neighbor's yard
my baseball slipped from my glove,

and when I knelt to retrieve it
I spied in a bare patch
a single black ant being torn to pieces
by a swarm of reds.

I couldn't look away.

DAY'S LABOR

He rises in darkness,
dons flannel, denim,
leather,

stands silent at the back screen,
spooning cereal from a bowl,
watching for first light.

Outside, waiting,
two saw horses, a nail bucket,
slender slats of pine.

Sunup to sundown
he measures and cuts,
hammers and planes,

not stopping to replenish,
never checking the cloudbank
threatening from the west,

until it's time to assemble,
long sides, short ends,
flat bottom, hinged top,

then climb in, lie down,
pull the lid closed over him,
trying it on for size.

VICTIM

after the Windsor Locks tornado, 1979

You are like the soldier
home from war in one piece,
left to hold his buddy's mother
as she clutches to her chest the folded flag:

the house across the way
has been wrenched from its foundation;
your home
stands.

Through the lengthening shadows of late afternoon
you help your neighbor sift through
the rubble of her life.
When it's too dark to see

you go home, straighten some lamp shades,
tape a few cracked windows,
without power
feel your way down the narrow hallway,
lie down fully clothed on your once familiar bed,

eyes wide open,
waiting for the light.

CHANGE

"Nine-eleven,"
she says, handing you the penny,
one dime, four ones and a five,
no recognition of what she's said
registering in her eyes
though it's only been weeks
since the towers fell.

You thank her,
pocket the coins
and start to slip the bills into your wallet,
when one of them catches your eye.
Around its edges
a message in bruise purple,
meticulous lettering,
all caps:
  "ALL GOOD THINGS SHALL COME TO ME
  FAR AWAY MISFORTUNE FLEE
  AS IT WILL SO MUST IT BE
  TEE HEE HEE HEE HEE HEE HEE!"

If it was September tenth,
when Anthrax was still just a metal band,
you would have smiled,
pictured some bored teen in a corner booth,
listlessly intent on scratching out a rhyme
while his girlfriend nibbled on the last of her fries,

but it's a different day,
so you scramble to the bathroom,

soap up your hands again and again,
then lift one corner of the bill
with a palmed paper towel
and slide it, silently,
into the stained metal can.

It's not until you walk outside
that you realize you haven't been breathing.
You look up.
The sky is a color you've never seen before.

THE LIFE-SIZED, CHAINSAWED MAGI OF STOWE, VERMONT

wait beside the manger,
a converted trough,
steps away from rough-hewn Mary and snub-nosed Joseph,
standing vigil.
No sign of a lamb, though,
or the ubiquitous donkey.

Instead, there are bear cubs holding signs
welcoming all who come equipped with American Express
and behind them an assemblage of God's wooden creatures:
deer of every size,
a sea of bull moose,
eagles in full flight,
Dutch boys, Sioux braves,
even a stallion twenty hands high,
regal beside a wigwam.
Just left of Joseph looms Carl Yastrzemski,
bat cocked,
taking dead aim at the slickered skull
of an unsuspecting lobsterman.

The magi are patient.
Like the rest of us
they've snaked their way north up Route 100,
convinced that if they give,
they'll get something in return.

VOCATIONAL EDUCATION

Seven p.m.
The students file in,
some in green,
most khaki.
All male.
This is Creative Writing for collegiate credit
at Somers Maximum Security Penitentiary,
but I don't feel secure,
and none of them look penitent
as we review the concept of narrative perspective.
They're here to tell their stories,
rewrite their lives,
the woman, this time, staying put where he told her,
the wheel man showing up
before the cops arrive,

no loose ends,
no hitches,
just bags full of money,
plane tickets out.

Nine o'clock.
Class dismissed.
I shovel papers into folders,
and start walking,
laminated pass visible at all times,
heels echoing,
machinery whirring
as the iron gates slide open before me,
slam shut behind.

I keep walking,
until I'm out the final doorway
in the well lit lot,
fingers clutching car keys all this time.

When the motor turns over
I slip it into gear
and head straight for the highway,
toward my waiting wife and son,
and tonight, especially,
our new baby girl.

V

THE DRUMMER AND
THE BUTTERFLY

Fortunately you carry along with you the higher-powered
reflective instrument that you can use
no matter how far down the road you've gone
to bring them back in view as large as life,
putting yourself in the picture, too, which makes
thinking about them as you saw them lasting.

Robert Shaw, "In the Rear-View Mirror"

UMPIRING MY SON'S LITTLE LEAGUE GAME

It blazes up and in,
head high.
He falls,

lies still,
right heel on home plate,
right cheek on the batter's box line.
On one knee beside him,
left hand on his hip,
I search his face for damage,
scan the crowd for help,
like the Kent State woman on the cover of *Time*.
No one
anywhere
is speaking.

Before I can move again
he's up,
fighting tears,
rotating his right shoulder,
whacking mud from the seat of his pants.
He nods to my every question,
then trots, head down, to first.

Polite, relieved applause.
"No one out," his coach reminds him.
"Forget about it," the catcher calls to his pitcher.
"That guy's run don't mean a thing."

FORT NIAGARA, FOURTH OF JULY

His uniform shirt white against the blue of Lake Ontario,
his 18 blue against that white.
Above it all his tanned face, smiling,
soccer ball tucked beneath one arm,
a state champ poised to tame New York.

When I take aim, Ontario vanishes
but for the slice between his lean, long legs,
legs that could easily span the great water,
one foot here,
the other in Toronto,
could straddle those skyscrapers
or crush them under foot,
like Godzilla in Tokyo,
if it suited his whim.

But then I see his other pose four days ago,
the one outside our hometown mall,
shoulders sagged,
chin in his chest,
arms invisible behind him.
To his right, his first date,
she, too, smaller
than when I dropped them off,
both of them shrunken
from running out of words
long before they planned.

When I take the camera away from my eye

he moves toward me,
larger with each stride,
puts his arm around my shoulder and says,
"When the tournament's over,
let's take a few more pictures
at the next Great Lake we find."

NANTUCKET FOG

Something out there pulses
the Atlantic over her toes,
yanks sand out from under her

out from under her again,
beats wet air hard
against her body,
eroding what was child
as she stands in sandy water,
T-shirt taut,
eyes fixed
on a spot known only to her,

as if expecting to sight
the cause of such relentlessness,
convinced it will breech
in astonishing suddenness,
or maybe inch its way,
teasingly,
withholding its identity
until the very last.

Either way,
she will stand her ground.
She will not turn away.

JUSTIN'S HANDS

"She was hit by the guy in the car right in front of us,
but he kept going, so we pulled over and got out,
and she was dead on someone's lawn, but there were babies,
two of them, they must've been inside her before she died,
and the first one didn't make it but the other …

so Jeff took off his shirt to wrap the live one, keep him warm
while Seth went home for help, and the rest of us kept taking
turns,
holding him,
stroking him.
He was trying to stand up like Bambi on the ice pond.
We all kept taking turns."

This he tells us in our kitchen after midnight,
his long percussive fingers rapping out a rhythm on his thighs,
but all I can see are his hands two months ago,
left one cupped at Nicky's purring chest,
right one stroking the length of his side.
At the lurch of the needle prick Justin's left holds fast
while his right maintains its gentle pace.
Nicky's breaths come slow, even,
in time with the calm, smooth strokes,
and then his final shudder,
his last release of air.

When at last he is ready,
Justin lets go,
stands,
jams both hands deep into jean pockets
like he's never going to take them out again.

NIGHTFALL, EARLY APRIL

Alone
behind her high school
beside the free-standing wall some use
for soccer practice
she lifts her slender brush.

Strawberry hair done up
to keep the paint off,
sweatshirt sleeves bunched above her elbows,
she crafts two swirling roses,
one for Jen
one for Asia.

One year.
One year
since her friends' car failed to hold the curve,
since she sped to the site
already strewn with flowers, small bears,
a rainbow of balloons,
since she wove among those gathered,
grabbing onto anyone, everyone,
anyone at all.

Daylight waning,
roses done
she steps back to gain perspective.
They'll do
as will the words that arch above them:
"In loving memory
Jen and Asia

You will always be with us
Forever young"

Head down
she makes her way
to her waiting car,
steps over white lines,
lands only in the empty spaces.

ON 81 SOUTH,
NEAR STAUNTON, VIRGINIA

Asleep since Hagerstown,
his long legs bent double,
knees planted in my seatback,
he finally shows signs of stirring.
He stretches as well as he can
in half of a back seat,
suitcase piled on suitcase
in the space behind his mom.
We are driving him to college,
from New England to the Old South.
It's late,
and there is hardly anyone on the road.

His face rises into the rear view mirror,
sleepy eyed,
cheeks flush,
long hair pulled taut
under his Yankee cap which faces backward,
as if to get a look at what it leaves behind.
And I think of how a minute ago
we were riding down Latimer Lane,
I pedaling, he strapped on in back,
the wind stinging my fingers through my gloves,
my thighs aching from the pull,
my heart struggling to keep pace,
until I stopped, unbuckled him,
and carried him with one arm,
the other guiding the handle bars home.

His headphones are on.
I hear the rhythm faintly
like the humming of a fly.
He lifts the earpiece away from one ear.
"I'm fine now, Dad, if you're tired.
Just find a spot to pull over and I'll drive."

FISH PUZZLE

Gone to hunt in Northampton for a graduation dress
she comes back, instead, brandishing a puzzle.
"It's all fish," she explains,
then sweeps toward her room.
The hum of her fan replaces the quiet,
next the first few notes of the latest Boyz II Men,
then the storm of five hundred laminated fish bits,
shaken loose from cardboard,
raining on her bed.

A half-hour later I lean against her door frame,
observe her sifting through signs.
At the center of the frame she's assembled before her
emptiness remains.
"This is hard, Daddy," she offers
without looking up

and I see her kneeling in the center of her playpen,
singing to herself,
clutching a red plastic ball,
then tugging it apart,
releasing the cascade of shapes trapped inside.
One by one she grasps triangles, rectangles,
octagons, stars,
slides each one smoothly through just the right hole
then chuckles as she lifts the ball
to set them free again.

The phone rings.
"Hello," she says,

cradling the receiver.
"Oh nothing," she adds.
As I ease into the hallway
she flops onto her back,
studying the box cover
an arm's length from her eyes
with its promise of shimmering pastel fluorescent fish,
perfect in their seamlessness
and headed her way.

MOWING ON MEMORIAL DAY

It's slow-going in this patch
that stretches from the deck to the full-grown maples,
thin grass thickened by overnight rain,
even slower in this one clump by the woodpile.
Here the motor chokes,
shies,
sputters to a stop.

When I yank the cord
there's only a whimper,
even less the next two tries,
so I weigh down the handle
and drop to one knee
to see what I need to dislodge.

Only when I straighten
do I recognize this spot:
it's where our cat is buried,

where two Mays ago my son unearthed
three feet of soil, dug deeper
than he had to, in spite of the heat,
in spite of the pain,
then nestled the box on the smooth, flat surface
he had leveled with the soles of his shoes.
The vet had offered to dispose of the remains,
but my son could only say,
"I have to know where he is."

I believed I would always think of Nicky

every time I set foot in this part of the yard,
but today I had forgotten,
as I'd done when I last mowed,
and perhaps the time before,

so I sit for a moment in the uncut grass,
lean my back against the woodpile
and describe for him the trellis
newly added to the garden,
tell him Lindsay has a job now,
Wednesday nights and Fridays,

and that Justin's nearly finished up
his first full year of college,
and in two weeks' time
he will be home.

TATTOO

She points to the nickel-sized
purple winged butterfly
and hands the man money to ink it
into the small of her back,
sufficiently fleshy,
not far from the bone.

It will follow her at summer's end
to her campus in the Catskills,
to classes and the cash machine,
to the quad where she will lie out
in the late September sun,
on excursions to Manhattan,
in and out of every alley shop Soho can provide,
along river banks in autumn dusk,
to the dining hall when hunger's tug
outweighs the winter wind,
and then back to us,
briefly,
at term's end.

You cannot give advice to a tattooed butterfly
or warn it what to watch for,
where to light
or when to fly,
but you can smile
when first you see
the arc its wings make,
and maybe touch it once for luck
with just the hollow of your hand.

THE PERCUSSIONIST

Was it his mother's heart
first taught him that everything, everywhere,
throbs with its own rhythm,
a beat he could divine
and echo with his hands?
That all of it, every chair arm, every handhold
on a school bus seatback, hell

even the Delta booth at Bradley International
has a pulse? No matter the inception,
it's continued to evolve these twenty-two years,
grown from spoons to Shostakovich,
from bathtub to Bartok.
So tonight, house dimmed down,

stage lights bright,
as he stands, tuxedoed, hands poised,
torso rising above the unstruck timpani,
it comes to me unbidden
with the certainty of sunrise

that even when those square shoulders
slump beneath the weight of winters
and I am in what darkened space there is to come,
he will take up his pair of 5A Pro Marks,
solid oak, wood tips,
sit down behind a sea of crashes
and pound those skins for everything he's worth,
beating time.

THIRD HOLE AT BUENA VISTA

for Diane

Head down, weight balanced,
she performs her standard practice swing
then steps up to the ball.

Once she's hit I tee it up,
draw back and unleash,
watch its flight as it peels off right,
headed for the pines.

Stomping away, I hear the wheels of her pull-cart
creak along the fairway,
then only the thumping of my heart.
When at last I find my ball
I yank out an iron,
doesn't matter which one,
and slash away.

I look back.
Head down, weight balanced,
she performs her standard practice swing
then steps up to the ball.

When we meet at the green
she says my last shot was perfect.
"I'm here in five," I grumble.

At the par three fourth
she sits on the bench

as the foursome ahead putts out.
I rub both palms hard against my pant legs,
angry at the sweat.

This time, when my first shot nestles
twenty feet from the flag,
we walk the fairway together.
"You hit yours solid," I tell her.
She smiles at me,
lifts her free hand to my collar,
smoothes out the twisted part
bunched against my neck.

EMPTY NEST

for Diane

She hangs it from the maple,
no more than a sapling twenty years ago,
now rounded to abundance.
From the same branch swings a feeder,
it, too, wren-sized,
designed to give access
only to the small.

The walls of this house are the color of balsa,
like the snap-together gliders
she'd assemble on a summer day,
then race up the steps to the highest porch
her apartment house provided,
determined that her creation
would have its best chance to fly.

Ever so gently, she lets go,
satisfied the maple's leaves
don't block the small, smooth O,
then strides to the sprinkler head,
re-directs its spray
so it arches to her garden,
to the new row of lilies,
to the single blazing star.

PHOTOGRAPH

The mailbox is yellow.
Both the driveway and the street
need new tar.
Looking over his right shoulder
he waves, the pioneer.
Incredible Hulk lunch box dangles at his knee,
protecting P&J on Wonder Bread,
Kool Aid in a Thermos, a snapshot of our cat.
Shoes stiff and sturdy,
dress navies pressed,
his white striped polo buttoned at the neck.
Above his squinting eyes a valance of hair,
not before or since so expertly combed.

To his left, her grin,
a full head shorter,
berry blonde curls wild with the heat.
Frozen against the school bus backdrop
she's rehearsing her departure,
her first real day of kindergarten
still two years away.

I look up from the opened album,
peer through the picture window
at the empty drive.
He's taken the white car to Creative Music,
she the gray to Misquamicut
for a lie-out in the sun.
Smooth dark tar

stretches to the humpbacked road.

I want to march across this blacktop
into the photograph,
gather them both with just one arm,
then slap the bus twice,
my sign to move on.

VI

AFTERWORD

WHEN POETRY IS KING

I will pause before the legend
MOST POPULAR COLLECTIONS,
wend my way deliciously
among burgeoning volumes.
What to choose...
What to choose...

Perhaps the new Olds,
one Rich or twin Doves,
or maybe a Hall I've always wanted to enter,
but most likely all of them,
one following the other,
each sweet plucked gingerly,
laid lovingly in the basket
swinging from my arm,

nor will I have to pay for them
(though each poet will be lavished with untold treasures
from the bottomless coffers of a hushed republic)
as I sweep to the egress,
stride out to the countryside,
where every tree bestows the exact amount of shade,
filters just enough sun
on the open golden pages.

Later, when I've turned the last leaf,
I'll look up, across the landscape.
At every tree a reader.
In every reader a light
that will never expire.

Steve Foley's poetry has appeared in publications such as *Northeast Magazine*, *Friends' Journal* and *The Portland Review*. His chapbook, *With the Hollow of Your Hand*, was published by Andrew Mountain Press in 1999. During the past twenty-five years he has given many poetry readings at venues such as the Sunken Garden Poetry Festival. Selected as 1980 Poet of the Year by the New England Association of Teachers of English, Foley has taught English and directed dramatic productions in Connecticut public high schools for more than three decades. He currently chairs the English Department of the High School and Middle School in South Windsor. He resides in Weatogue, Connecticut with his wife, Diane, an elementary school teacher. They are the parents of Justin, a professional musician, and Lindsay, a speech pathologist.

To order additional copies
of *A Place at the Table*
or other Antrim House titles
contact the publisher at

Antrim House
P.O. Box 111
Tariffville, CT 06081
860-217-0023
www.antrimhousebooks.com
eds@antrimhousebooks.com